May 2019

The Top Six

/// THREATS

to Civilization

# GLOBAL WARMING

Erin L. McCoy

Cavendish
Square

New York

Published in 2019 by Cavendish Square Publishing, LLC
243 5th Avenue, Suite 136, New York, NY 10016

Library of Congress Cataloging-in-Publication Data
Names: McCoy, Erin L., author.
Title: Global warming / Erin L. McCoy.
Description: First edition. | New York : Cavendish Square, [2018] |
Series: The top six threats to civilization | Audience: Grades 5 to 8. |
Includes bibliographical references and index.
Identifiers: LCCN 2018026119 (print) | LCCN 2018026381 (ebook) |
ISBN 9781502640765 (ebook) | ISBN 9781502640758 (library bound) |
ISBN 9781502640741 (pbk.)
Subjects: LCSH: Global warming–Juvenile literature. |
Climatic changes–Effect of human beings on–Juvenile literature. |
Greenhouse effect, Atmospheric–Juvenile literature.
Classification: LCC QC981.8.G56 (ebook) | LCC QC981.8.G56 M38985 2018 (print) |
DDC 363.738/74–dc23
LC record available at https://lccn.loc.gov/2018026119

Editorial Director: David McNamara
Copy Editor: Alex Tessman
Associate Art Director: Alan Sliwinski
Designer: Ginny Kemmerer
Production Coordinator: Karol Szymczuk
Photo Research: J8 Media

Portions of this book originally appeared in *Catastrophic Climate
Change and Global Warming* by Frank Spalding.

Printed in the United States of America

# CONTENTS

# INTRODUCTION:
# A WORLD IN PERIL

Imagine: fifty years from now, the city of Miami, Florida, is completely underwater—and so are dozens of other coastal cities throughout the United States and around the world. Residents have fled inland, leaving many of their belongings behind. Millions have been displaced—so many that the president has declared a national emergency. Shelters have been set up in high school gymnasiums and sports arenas. Americans are donating food and blankets, but these displaced Miami residents have lost their homes and their jobs, and it will take a long time for many of them to get back on their feet.

Within a few years, the national unemployment rate has increased dramatically. As many coastal cities have succumbed to flooding due to rising sea levels, the country has also witnessed the disappearance of millions of jobs. Now, an economic recession is underway. Millions more people are living in poverty, and the federal government is struggling to fund them. At the same time, the government is investing billions of dollars to build levees and remodel cities in an attempt to prevent more communities from sinking underwater.

*Opposite*: After heavy rains, pedestrians and cars make their way through the streets of Miami, Florida, on August 1, 2017. Miami is projected to eventually be completely underwater as a result of rising global temperatures.

# CATASTROPHIC LOSSES

For many, it is still hard to believe that just a few degrees' increase in the average global temperature could cause so much turmoil. Yet this hypothetical picture of our world's future, dismal as it is, is quite possible. Take a look at our environment fifty years from now: glaciers at the poles and around the world are melting; there aren't any left in Glacier National Park in Montana. Melting permafrost has released large amounts of the greenhouse gas methane into the air, speeding up the process of global warming. Many of Earth's rain forests, which

The release of carbon dioxide and other greenhouse gases into the air is a major contributing factor to human-caused climate change.

once helped slow the greenhouse effect by absorbing the greenhouse gas carbon dioxide, have been destroyed to make room for farmland.

Oceans have become more acidic, and marine animals such as fish, dolphins, and jellyfish are dying off in large numbers. Polar bears have gone extinct, many having drowned as they swam frantically in search of ice to land on. Also extinct are multiple species of sea turtles, the Adélie penguin, and the ringed seal. Coral reefs, which are more diverse communities than even rain forests, have all but died out, as have the plants and animals that once lived there.

These are tragic losses in themselves, but they're also devastating to human communities, who rely on these animals to maintain a delicate ecological balance. Butterflies and other pollinators will suffer, meaning crops might not be fertilized, causing widespread agricultural failures. With the temperature increase, fundamental elements of local ecosystems throughout the world—from wind patterns to precipitation—will change, so that crops that could once grow in certain areas no longer can. Widespread starvation and migration ensues. People seek to build new lives elsewhere, but those who have spent their lives farming no longer know how to cultivate crops in these new areas—or on the very lands they once knew so well. Catastrophic climate change has also resulted in increasing rates of cancer from ultraviolet (UV) radiation.

## REAL DANGERS

Just how possible are such scenarios? Are the effects of global warming overblown? Some argue that we have little or nothing to worry about—that the Earth's temperature has gone up and down many times over the last 4.5 billion years. However, past changes have generally occurred much more gradually, as the result of naturally occurring events.

This time, many argue, is different. Human industrial development paired with rapid population increases have created conditions never before seen in the history of the planet. Greenhouse gases are being released at record rates, not only through industrial and vehicle emissions, but as carbon dioxide–storing forests are cut down to make way for development. A paper published in the *Anthropocene Review* in 2017 found that human-caused climate change is 170 times faster than change caused by natural factors. And while some claim that scientists disagree on whether human-caused climate change is real, multiple studies have shown that at least 97 percent of climate scientists who are actively publishing agree that it is "extremely likely" that humans have caused the climate to warm over the last hundred years.

In fact, many scenarios that sound extreme are in fact extremely possible, according to climate-change scientists. The World Wildlife Fund reported in 2018 that in the globe's most naturally diverse areas, such as rain forests and the Galapagos Islands, up to 50 percent of all animal and plant species are at risk as a result of climate change. Even if moderate temperature-increase projections come true, these areas may lose 25 percent of the species living there. More than sixteen thousand species are already listed by the International Union for Conservation of Nature (IUCN) as endangered. The number of threatened species includes 25 percent of mammals, roughly one in eight birds, 41 percent of amphibians, 33 percent of reef-building corals, and 70 percent of all plants, according to the IUCN. While global warming is not the only cause of species endangerment, it has played a large role.

Projected impacts on humans are also severe. As of late 2017, projections estimate that by 2100, global temperatures will have increased 5.8 degrees Fahrenheit (3.2 degrees Celsius) above preindustrial levels. According to nonprofit organization Climate Central, about 275 million people currently live in places that, at a 5.4°F (3°C) increase, will be underwater. This includes the entire city of Miami, Florida, and in fact, even at 3.6°F (2°C), nearly the whole southern third of the state of Florida, home to seven million people. It also includes the city of Shanghai, China, where 17.5 million people would be displaced; Hong Kong, China, with 8.4 million affected; Osaka, Japan, 5.2 million; Rio de Janeiro, Brazil, 1.8 million; and Alexandria, Egypt,

3 million. Four of New York City's five boroughs would be threatened by chronic flooding. Meanwhile, the World Food Programme (WFP) estimates that the increasing frequency and intensity of such natural disasters as storms, floods, and droughts could increase the global risk of hunger and malnutrition by 20 percent by 2050. Climate-related disasters have already cost the WFP $23 billion in the last decade.

Still, there is hope. Agencies and governments throughout the world have recognized the threat of global warming and are implementing policies to either slow it down or reduce its impact. Every individual has a role to play in improving the health of the planet, and if everyone works together toward a common goal, we can make a change for the better.

# CHAPTER 1
## HUMAN-CAUSED CLIMATE CHANGE

**W**hile the term "climate change" can refer to both naturally occurring and human-caused transformations, the term "global warming" almost always refers to those increases in temperature caused by humans. Global warming is just one key component of the many changes the planet is now undergoing. Climate change refers to the effects—both direct and indirect—of global warming and other changes. These effects include droughts, more intense natural disasters, flooding, and ocean acidification.

Scientists around the world have been working to understand the many factors contributing to accelerating climate change, and what consequences we have seen or might expect to see. A deeper knowledge of both cause and effect will teach us what each of us can do to protect the planet.

## SCIENTIFIC CERTAINTY

Science has helped us both understand the natural world and examine our impact on it. Scientists first took notice of Earth's gradual warming approximately one hundred years ago. At that time, the extent of our

Above: On August 19, 2014—three years into a major drought—parts of Lake Oroville in California were nearly dry. Water levels in reservoirs and lakes were at historic lows.

The amount of greenhouse gases and other pollution being released into the environment increased during the Industrial Revolution, shown here at its height in nineteenth-century England.

impact on the world was not entirely clear. The first serious research into global warming began about fifty years ago.

As scientists began to realize that Earth's climate was changing mainly due to human activities, people around the world became concerned. In 1988, the United Nations Environment Programme and the World Meteorological Organization formed a group to study global warming. This organization, the Intergovernmental Panel on Climate Change (IPCC), is the most significant body of experts ever convened to examine the effects of climate change. The IPCC assesses climate data and scientific reports from hundreds of scientists around the world to produce neutral, objective reports on the state of the world's climate. In 2007, the IPCC won the Nobel Peace Prize for its work. That same year, the panel released a report concluding that there was no question that global warming was occurring, and it was almost certainly being caused by human activity.

Why "almost certainly"? It is important to understand that in science, it is sometimes considered essentially impossible to have absolute certainty. When it comes to understanding the climate of the Earth, for instance, there will always be some uncertainty; there are simply too many factors to test, too many experiments that could be run, too many things to know. If a scientist claimed she understood the climate "completely," she would close the door to future experimentation and discoveries. The idea that, because there is uncertainty, human-caused climate change is probably not happening at all reflects a common misunderstanding about how science works. Pundits point to this lack of certainty without realizing that it is an essential part of the scientific process.

The same holds true regarding predictions about climate change. It is, after all, impossible to predict the future with 100 percent accuracy, no matter the scenario. However, when scientists say that they have a "very high confidence" that their projections for the future are true, that means that their prediction has at least a 90 percent chance of occurring. When it comes to predicting the future, you have to be pretty certain to say that. And after all, uncertainty around the future trajectory of climate change largely stems from not knowing what choices humans will or won't make to protect the planet.

Still, there are many facts that scientists are, indeed, certain about. "We have learned, for example, that the burning of fossil fuels and the clearing of forests release carbon dioxide ($CO_2$) into the atmosphere. There is no uncertainty about this," writes the Union of Concerned Scientists. "We have learned that carbon dioxide and other greenhouse gases in the atmosphere trap heat through the greenhouse effect. Again, there is no uncertainty about this."

# THE INDUSTRIAL REVOLUTION

It is believed that humanity's impact on the global climate is tied to one of our greatest achievements: the Industrial Revolution. During the Industrial Revolution, which began during the mid-eighteenth century in England and continued through the mid-nineteenth century, new technologies changed the way that people in the Western world lived and worked. Agricultural advances made the mass production of food possible for the first time. New technology also allowed people to mass-produce goods like textiles and machine parts in factories. Railroads changed how people traveled, and the telegraph revolutionized communication. These great technological advances soon spread around the world. People began to rapidly modernize cities, where they sought jobs in the emerging industries created by these new technologies.

Today, industrialized production makes our way of life possible. Our stores are full of affordable toys, clothes, and household goods made in factories across the globe. Regardless of the season, supermarkets in the United States are stuffed with a dazzling variety of exotic and international fresh foods. Cars and other modes of personal transportation are abundant and affordable. Advances in science and medicine have allowed us to enjoy a much longer lifespan. We have also achieved a much higher average standard of living than at any other time in history.

In the mid-twentieth century, scientists began assessing the impact of all this industrialized human activity on the environment. Fossil fuels such as coal and oil might power factories and transportation, but they also release carbon dioxide into the air. Livestock in large industrialized farms provide the world with food, but they also release a great deal of methane into the atmosphere. There are many human activities that release these and other greenhouse gases into the air. Ultimately, these emissions lead to climate change.

# THE GREENHOUSE EFFECT

To understand how human beings can affect the climate, we first have to understand a natural process known as the greenhouse effect. The greenhouse effect is an important natural process that existed well before human beings first appeared on the planet. In fact, it makes life on Earth possible.

When sunlight passes through the atmosphere and reaches our planet's surface, some of its energy is absorbed by the Earth. The sunlight warms the Earth's surface, and this causes infrared radiation to be released. Some of this radiation exits through the atmosphere,

## Greenhouse effect

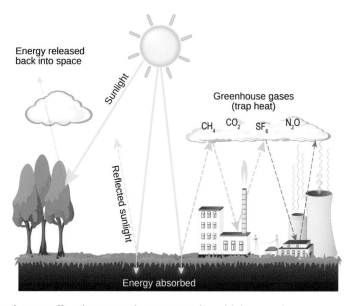

The greenhouse effect is a complex process by which greenhouse gases trap heat in the atmosphere.

vanishing into space—but some of it is trapped by certain greenhouse gases present in our atmosphere, such as carbon dioxide ($CO_2$). The energy trapped by greenhouse gases warms the atmosphere, in turn causing Earth's surface temperatures to rise.

Without the greenhouse effect, Earth would be too cold to sustain life. However, if the greenhouse effect spins out of control and begins trapping too much heat, it might warm the planet too much. Consider Earth's neighbors Mars and Venus. The greenhouse effect is negligible on Mars. As a consequence, the planet is too cold for human life. On Venus, however, the greenhouse effect is very pronounced. The surface of that planet is so hot that it would cause any known life-form to evaporate instantly.

It may seem incredible that human beings have the power to alter our planet's natural greenhouse effect—but it appears that we do. About 1 percent of Earth's atmosphere is made up of greenhouse gases. These include carbon dioxide, methane, nitrous oxide, and water vapor, among others. The greenhouse effect currently keeps Earth's average temperature at 59°F (15°C)—already 1.62°F (0.9°C) higher than the average between 1951 and 1980. An increase in the amount of greenhouse gases in the atmosphere can cause the greenhouse effect to increase. The end result is that temperatures on Earth's surface also rise.

## GREENHOUSE GASES

In the United States, approximately 30 percent of all electricity is generated by coal. Another 32 percent is derived from natural gas. When coal and natural gas burn, they release greenhouse gases into the atmosphere. In fact, all fossil fuels release greenhouse gases when they burn. Greenhouse gases are also released by livestock (such as

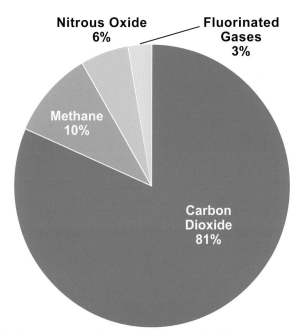

## U.S. Greenhouse Gas Emissions in 2016

Nitrous Oxide
6%

Fluorinated
Gases
3%

Methane
10%

Carbon
Dioxide
81%

U.S. Environmental Protection Agency (2018). Inventory of U.S.
Greenhouse Gas Emissions and Sinks: 1990-2016

In 2016, the United States released 6.5 billion metric tons of greenhouse gases. Shown on the pie graph above are the types of gases that were emitted.

cows, sheep, and pigs), landfills, and melting permafrost. The United States is the world's second-largest producer of greenhouse gases, surpassed only by China.

Currently, there are about 7.6 billion human beings on Earth. By the year 2040, it is estimated that there could be as many as 9 billion. To put this in perspective, the world's human population was only about 3 billion in 1960. Human activity creates greenhouse gases.

# Atmosphere

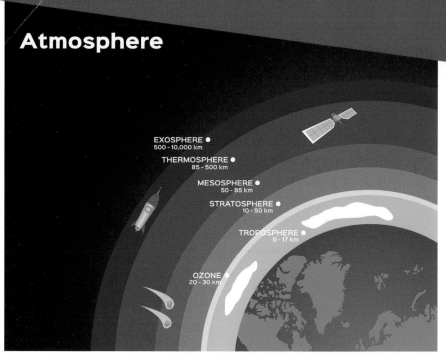

EXOSPHERE ●
500 - 10,000 km

THERMOSPHERE ●
85 - 500 km

MESOSPHERE ●
50 - 85 km

STRATOSPHERE ●
10 - 50 km

TROPOSPHERE ●
0 - 17 km

OZONE ●
20 - 30 km

The Earth's atmosphere is comprised of multiple layers, each with its own unique characteristics.

The more humans there are, the more greenhouse gases are released into the atmosphere.

## CARBON DIOXIDE

Carbon dioxide, or $CO_2$, comprises 76 percent of all greenhouse gas emissions on the planet. When you breathe in oxygen, you exhale carbon dioxide. The carbon dioxide exhaled by humans and animals is absorbed by plants, which use it to photosynthesize. During photosynthesis, plants use the energy of sunlight to convert carbon dioxide into sugars and other organic compounds. At the end of this process, plants emit oxygen, which humans and animals breathe, beginning the cycle all over again. This process is part of a phenomenon known as the carbon cycle.

The carbon cycle is one of the processes that keep Earth's atmosphere, oceans, and land balanced and healthy. Plants help remove carbon dioxide from the atmosphere, reducing the levels of the heat-trapping

# Natural Cycles

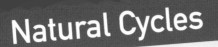

The planet has experienced several ice ages throughout history as a result of a fluctuation in Earth's average temperatures over time.

Twenty thousand years ago, Earth's climate was much cooler than it is today. Scientists refer to this period as an "ice age." During the ice age, most of North America was covered with large sheets of glacial ice.

Earth's temperature fluctuates over time in a sort of cycle. Ice ages have occurred periodically throughout Earth's history. Some have lasted for tens of millions of years. During some of the warmer periods between ice ages, conditions were warmer than they are today. Changes in Earth's temperature may be caused by a number of factors, including changes in solar radiation, the composition of atmospheric gases, and ocean circulation.

As scientists understand more about Earth's past climate changes, they are better able to project how our climate might change in the future. Today, scientists are mostly concerned with how human activity can affect the natural cycle of temperature fluctuation.

gas that can build up there. In addition to absorbing potentially harmful carbon dioxide, plants supply us with life-giving oxygen. When this carbon cycle is disrupted, global warming is the result.

Fossil fuels are composed of carbon that has been stored in the Earth for millions of years. It is believed that they're made from the compressed remains of ancient zooplankton and algae, which was composed of carbon—the building block of all life. Fossil fuels are responsible for about 90 percent of the world's energy. When fossil fuels are burned, this carbon—which has been stored for millions of years within the planet and thus has been kept out of the atmosphere where it would trap heat—is suddenly released into the atmosphere. Human beings release nearly ten billion metric tons of carbon a year into the atmosphere, about twenty times more than in 1990. More than half of this is eventually absorbed by vegetation. The rest, however, lingers in the atmosphere, trapping heat.

Vegetation plays a crucial role in regulating Earth's climate. Unfortunately, large swaths of forest are cut down every day. Whether it's to provide wood for construction or to create fields for farming, the destruction of Earth's tree and plant life is bad news. Deforestation results in there being less vegetation to take part in the carbon cycle, meaning that more of this carbon dioxide remains in the atmosphere, trapping heat and altering the climate.

## METHANE AND NITROUS OXIDE

The greenhouse gas methane comprises 16 percent of all greenhouse gas emissions. Methane is emitted by a number of natural sources, such as soil deposits, animal emissions (the release of gas and solid waste), swamps, and oceans. These processes account for approximately one-half the amount of methane released into the atmosphere. Human beings generate the rest. Activities such as refining natural gas and other fossil fuels, processing wastewater, rice farming, and the raising of livestock all produce methane. A great deal of methane is also generated when organic matter decays. This means that swamps and wetlands release methane, as do our massive landfills (garbage dumps).

Human activities such as agriculture, the burning of fossil fuels, and waste processing also produce the greenhouse gas nitrous oxide.

## OTHER GREENHOUSE GASES

Ozone is a greenhouse gas as well, but it has varying effects at different levels of the atmosphere. High up in the stratosphere, ozone is helpful. The ozone layer blocks UV light, which can cause sunburn and, over time, skin cancer. However, lower down, in the troposphere, ozone is a pollutant. It is harmful to people with respiratory problems, and it traps heat.

Other greenhouse gases are very damaging to the ozone layer. These are high–global warming potential (GWP) gases. They are not released in as great a quantity as other greenhouse gases, but their effect on the atmosphere can be much more serious. High-GWP gases are generated by many industrial processes, such as aluminum manufacturing. Although there has been a widespread effort to limit their use in the United States, high-GWP gas emissions have been steadily climbing.

## FEEDBACK

There are many ways that people produce greenhouse gas emissions. Global warming and climate change are complicated, however. Gauging the impact of climate change is more complicated than simply measuring the degree of pollution that human beings pump into the atmosphere. The causes of climate change can create a feedback loop that actually worsens the effect of global warming. What this means is that our activities can set in motion larger consequences that create a sort of snowball effect.

What is feedback? Feedback describes a unique cause-and-effect relationship. In climate science, the word "feedback" describes how a seemingly small shift in climate can cause far more dramatic climate changes. For instance, glacial ice reflects sunlight back into outer space, beyond our atmosphere. This reflected sunlight is not absorbed by Earth. This means that it doesn't generate infrared radiation that can be trapped by greenhouse gases. The rise in temperatures on Earth's surface in recent decades, however, has resulted in the reduction in size and extent of the planet's ice masses. The less ice there is to reflect sunlight, the more infrared radiation the Earth absorbs and emits back into the atmosphere, where it becomes trapped by the greenhouse gases, resulting in more climate change and more ice melting—and so the loop continues.

These feedback loops are complex, and it's not always easy to recognize them or understand the full extent of their effect. They are, however, particularly worrisome, since they can accelerate the impacts of climate change. Because of such loops, even small actions can have a big impact. That's why we can't rely on international efforts alone; it is also essential for individuals to make small, daily efforts to conserve the planet.

# CHAPTER 2
## DEVASTATING IMPACTS

A warmer planet doesn't mean the end of winter, universally balmier weather, and more days to spend at the beach—not at all, in fact. While the Earth's average annual temperature as a whole will increase, weather patterns won't be any more uniform than they are now. Some places will get hotter than others, including areas that are already hot enough as it is. When temperature patterns change this quickly, there are many more negative effects than there are positive.

It is widely believed that the weather will become more unpredictable, with an increase in dangerous, destructive, and deadly storms. Heat waves will cause people to die in the summer months. Diseases that thrive in warmer weather may spread to regions of the world where they previously could not have survived. Oceans will become more acidic, and their levels will rise, swallowing miles and miles of coastal land and entire islands. There will be famines, water shortages, and droughts. These changes will prove to be deadly for many species of animals—and possibly human beings as well.

Above: Hurricane Irma slams into Miami, Florida, with its 100-mile-per-hour (160-kilometer-per-hour) winds in 2017.

# EXTREME WEATHER

Global climate change might lead to stronger hurricanes and tornadoes. Severe storms can kill thousands of people and cause millions, if not billions, of dollars in property damage. Currently, the United States experiences an average of more than a thousand tornadoes a year. Places such as the Netherlands, Australia, Bangladesh, New Zealand, South Africa, and the United Kingdom are also prone to tornado activity, though they have many fewer than the United States. While some tornadoes last for more than an hour, most only last ten minutes or less. Still, even a short-lived tornado can create catastrophic damage, destruction, and death.

The deadliest tornado in US history occurred in March 1925. It was known as the Tri-State Tornado. It was so named because it passed through Missouri, Illinois, and Indiana. By the time the Tri-State Tornado had dissipated, 695 people had been killed. This is not the deadliest tornado on record, however. Tornadoes in Bangladesh have been even more deadly. A 1989 storm killed more than one thousand people there, causing enormous devastation.

Tornadoes can produce winds that generally range from 40 to 110 miles per hour (64 to 177 kilometers per hour). If a serious one were to touch down in a major US city—such as Chicago, Illinois, for instance, which is in a "tornado alley"—the damage could be staggering, causing millions of dollars in damages. Even worse, tens of thousands of people could be killed. The United States has more tornadoes than any other country in the world. It will be hit particularly hard if global warming produces more numerous and powerful storms.

Meanwhile, the Geophysical Fluid Dynamics Laboratory (GFDL) predicts that tropical cyclones (that is, both hurricanes and typhoons) will be 2–11 percent more intense by the end of the twenty-first century as a result of human contributors. Rainfall within such storms may increase 10–15 percent. "This change would imply an even larger percentage increase in the destructive potential per storm, assuming no reduction in storm size," the GFDL reports.

## RISING SEA LEVELS

There is a great deal of glacial ice on Earth. This ice helps regulate and moderate the planet's temperature by reflecting the sun's rays back into space. Ice also stores much of the world's fresh water. With global warming, as surface temperatures increase and the ice melts, Earth's

Ice breaks off from the Perito Moreno Glacier in Patagonia, Argentina, in a process called "calving."

# Threatening a Way of Life

An Inuit hunter on Baffin Island, Canada, hunts seals on an ice floe. Changing global temperatures have disrupted the Inuits' way of life.

Living largely within the Arctic Circle, the Inuit people have existed in harmony with their environment for centuries. However, a warming climate has increasingly disrupted their way of life. Melting permafrost is causing roads and buildings to sink and collapse, as the land they are built on is no longer completely frozen.

Meanwhile, erratic weather has changed the migration patterns of animals such as caribou, whales, and seals that the Inuit traditionally hunt. These changes have made them more reliant on less-healthy and much more expensive store-bought food. As a result, seven in ten Inuit children in Nunavut, Canada, live in households where food can be hard to come by. The Inuit are worried that, should climate change continue at its current pace, their entire way of life could disappear.

seas will rise. This will endanger many islands and coastal communities, as well as the world's many cities that are built near water. New York, New Orleans, Amsterdam, and many other cities could be submerged as sea levels rise. Miles of valuable coastline could be lost. Small island nations that are only a few feet above sea level could be completely submerged. People living in these areas would have to move, creating mass migrations and strains on resources in the countries to which they flee. Businesses and industries will have to be shut down, and either relocate or disappear altogether.

Rising seas can contaminate freshwater sources, such as lakes and rivers, with salt. Should a tipping point be reached, the large amounts of ice contained in Antarctica and Greenland could melt, which would be disastrous. Polar bears that count on polar ice are already seeing their habitats destroyed. In fact, scientists are finding that polar bears are already drowning as they swim greater and greater distances between ice floes and sheets where they hunt and rest. They are an endangered species.

Ice isn't only found floating in the ocean. There are large areas of Earth where the ground is frozen year-round. This is known as permafrost. Trillions of metric tons of organic matter are frozen solid in Earth's permafrost. The warming of the globe is causing this permafrost to thaw. Permafrost stores a great amount of carbon. When it thaws, this carbon is released into the atmosphere. These vast stores of carbon, if released, could mark a dramatic and sudden contribution to global warming. In East Siberia alone, it is estimated that there are 500 gigatons (1,100 trillion pounds) of frozen carbon reserves. As discussed earlier, this can begin a feedback effect—the carbon released from the melting permafrost contributes to global warming, which then causes more permafrost to melt, which releases more carbon, and the cycle perpetuates itself. If all of our permafrost thaws, the results could be disastrous.

## HEAT WAVES

In 2003, a brutal heat wave descended on Europe. Temperatures were higher than they had been in years. It is believed that these high temperatures can be directly linked to the effect that human beings have on global climate. While it is impossible to pinpoint exactly how many people died as a result of the heat wave, it's believed that about thirty thousand deaths can be attributed to it. Nearly fifteen thousand people died in France alone.

On a particularly hot day in Paris, France, people splash in the Trocadero fountain to cool off. Thousands of deaths were attributed to this 2003 heat wave in Europe.

Extremely hot weather is especially dangerous to the elderly. When the human body senses that it is overheating, it works overtime to maintain a safe core temperature. This can put a great strain on elderly bodies. Often, the elderly are less aware of the heat. They don't feel it as acutely as younger people do, so they may not take precautions to cool themselves down, such as seeking out fans, air conditioners, and cool drinks.

Record-high temperatures were noted in many countries in 2003. If the decades-long trend holds, it appears that temperatures will just keep rising. Will it get too hot for people to survive someday? Some climate scientists think this is a distinct possibility, especially in certain parts of the world where heat, disease, famine, drought, and desertification will become extreme. Hosmay Lopez, meteorologist and lead author of a study published in *Nature Climate Change* in 2018, says, "Without human influence, half of the extreme heat waves projected to occur in the future wouldn't happen."

# DROUGHT, FAMINE, AND DISEASE

It's possible that higher temperatures and changing weather patterns will cause widespread drought. This, in turn, could lead to massive famine. There are places in the world, such as the southwestern United States and southern Africa, which are particularly sensitive to drought conditions. Hundreds of millions of people could be affected by diminished water supplies. They could be forced to migrate to find water, which could create conflicts in the communities that they pass through or settle in.

Coupled with the rapidly increasing human population, serious water shortages could be fatal for large groups of people. As land dries up and turns into desert, there may not be enough water to provide

International aid organization Oxfam distributes water during a drought in the Horn of Africa in 2011.

irrigation to grow food. Right now, 99 percent of all water is not fit for human consumption. The remaining 1 percent is not available to everyone on Earth. According to Water.org, an organization that has brought sanitation and safe water to twelve million people, 844 million individuals lack access to safe water. A child dies every ninety seconds as a result of a water-related disease, and one million people die every year. If climate change continues as projected, this number may increase. Human beings simply cannot live without access to clean and reliable freshwater supplies.

Changing temperatures not only put more people at risk for waterborne diseases, but for other diseases, as well. Certain temperatures support certain organisms better than others. Some fear that a warming globe will encourage the spread of tropical diseases, which thrive in warmer temperatures, into new regions of the globe. In a worst-case scenario, this could pose a potentially fatal danger to billions of people who have not built up natural defenses against these diseases.

# SPECIES EXTINCTION

Many animals are very sensitive to changes in their ecosystems. If global warming alters those ecosystems, they may be unable to survive. Changing temperatures will almost certainly cause many species to vanish. More than a million species worldwide could be in danger of extinction.

The increase in atmospheric carbon has made the oceans more acidic. The oceans absorb a great deal of atmospheric carbon—up to 25.4 million metric tons every day. The more carbon we pump into the

Nearly all sea turtle species are endangered due to loss of habitat, hunting, and/or climate change. This includes the hawksbill turtle, shown here, which is critically endangered.

An estimated 98 percent of coral reefs will be suffering stress that results in bleaching, shown here, by 2050. Bleaching occurs when coral expels the symbiotic algae that lives in its tissue, causing it to turn white. This process does not necessarily kill the coral, but often does.

atmosphere, the more the oceans absorb, and the more acidic they get. Ocean acidity is harmful to many types of marine life, such as corals, plankton, and marine snails. If organisms at the bottom of the food chain, such as plankton, die out, what will happen to the organisms that eat them? By 2100, the oceans could become too acidic to support a great deal of marine life. Ocean life—one of this planet's great wonders, natural resources, and food sources—could be virtually decimated, and oceans could be dull, lifeless expanses of acidic water.

Sea turtle species, nearly all of which are already endangered, are likely to suffer the effects of changing sea currents, and warming sands may cause more of their eggs to hatch females, leading to an imbalance that may prevent them from breeding. Ringed seals, which give birth on icebergs, are in danger when these icebergs break apart, separating babies from their mothers. Melting nest sites and sea-temperature changes that have reduced fish populations have also endangered the Adélie penguin. These are just a few of countless ocean species being threatened.

Species of coral are at particularly high risk. Coral reefs, often called "rain forests of the sea," provide shelter and food for a huge variety of other plants and animals. These reefs are extremely sensitive to temperature changes. Critically endangered staghorn coral species in the Bahamas, Florida, and the Gulf of Mexico have already declined by as much as 98 percent since the 1980s. As Patrick Barkham wrote in the *Guardian* newspaper in 2017:

> Since 2005, the Caribbean region has lost 50% of its corals, largely because of rising sea temperatures and mass bleaching incidents which have killed coral around the world … Across the world, coral reefs are bleaching and dying: Japan's government this year reported that almost three-quarters of its biggest coral reef has died, blaming rising sea temperatures caused by global warming. Australia's Great Barrier Reef experienced the worst bleaching ever recorded by scientists in 2016.

The US National Oceanic and Atmospheric Administration predicts that 98 percent of coral reefs around the world will be suffering the impacts of bleaching-level thermal stress by 2050.

Land-based species are just as much at risk because of global warming. The Sierra Nevada blue, a butterfly endemic to Spain, is already endangered, and many other pollinators essential to the perpetuation of plant life, including bees, may be put at risk too. The giant mountain lobelia, a spiky alpine plant native to Ethiopia, will find just 3.4 percent of its preferred habitat still inhabitable by 2080. In the world's most naturally diverse and rich areas—from the Galapagos Islands to the Amazon rain forest—as many as half of all plant and animal species will be threatened by climate change, the World Wildlife Fund reported in 2018.

Climate change is a complicated web of causes and effects. While we know many of the factors that increase global warming, the extent of their impact is sometimes difficult to predict. To complicate matters, many people in politics and in the media argue that the climate change we are seeing now is not caused by humans. Very few of those who hold these opinions have any background in climate science. In order to take a rational look at climate change, then, we must carefully review the scientific evidence.

There are things that we can do to lessen our impact on the atmosphere, and there are ways that we can adapt our lifestyles to a changing world. While we are still working to fully understand the phenomenon of climate change, we have already learned enough to predict, with some certainty, what the future will hold. This knowledge can help us learn how to prepare for and adapt to our changing climate.

## A PANEL OF EXPERTS

Formed in 1988, the Intergovernmental Panel on Climate Change (IPCC) is a source of objective and nonpartisan research into climate change. The organization assesses climate data from hundreds of

Above: With ice melting much sooner than usual, many polar bears such as this one are unable to migrate to where they can find food, and ultimately starve.

scientists around the world. After processing this data, it produces reports summarizing the findings.

The most recent IPCC report was released in 2014, and it was one of the most definitive reports on climate change ever produced. By drawing from such a wide variety of sources, the IPCC has produced some of the most thorough, accurate, and compelling research into climate change. It confirmed "that human influence on the climate system is clear and growing, with impacts observed across all continents and oceans." The IPCC declared 95 percent certainty that humans are the primary cause of the global warming that we are seeing today. What's more, it reported that meeting the commonly stated goal of keeping the temperature increase at 5.6°F (2°C) above preindustrial levels "will require an urgent and fundamental departure from business as usual."

Two men paddle through the Ninth Ward neighborhood of New Orleans, Louisiana, after Hurricane Katrina flooded much of the city in 2005. Coastal cities such as New Orleans face the dual threat of rising sea levels and more intense weather events as a result of global warming.

A 2017 report—"the most comprehensive study ever of climate science by U.S. government researchers," according to NPR—called human activities the "dominant cause" of global warming and said that the last 115 years have been "the warmest in the history of modern civilization." The "Climate Science Special Report" was authored by experts from such scientific agencies as the Department of Energy, the National Aeronautics and Space Administration (NASA), and the National Oceanic and Atmospheric Administration. In fact, without major changes, the global temperature might increase to as much as 9°F (5°C) above preindustrial levels.

# GLOBAL EFFECTS

With almost complete certainty, it is now known that average global temperatures will increase throughout the twenty-first century and beyond. We also know that human beings are contributing to this temperature increase.

According to the IPCC, there have been fewer cold days and more heat waves over the last fifty years than at any other time since temperatures have been recorded. Furthermore, the temperatures of the last fifty years were, on average, the highest in the Northern Hemisphere since at least 1000 CE. The IPCC believes that this warming can be directly traced back to human activity. The five warmest years on record have all taken place during the 2010s, and it can only be assumed that the record-breaking temperatures being recorded now will be surpassed in the near future.

Snow and ice cover around the world have decreased. Many ancient glaciers will not survive the twenty-first century. High temperatures have caused sea ice in the Arctic to melt at a rate of approximately 2.7 percent

A part of the Amazon rain forest in Brazil has been cleared to make way for soybean crops. Deforestation increases the amount of greenhouse gases in the air.

per decade since 1978. This melting ice has caused, and will continue to cause, sea levels to rise. In Antarctica, large chunks of ice have broken free of the main Antarctic ice mass. For instance, in 2017, an iceberg the size of the state of Delaware broke free of Antarctica. Scientists report that there is little evidence that this particular break was connected with human-caused climate change, though some say that it could have made the break more likely. Ice shelves melt quicker in the open ocean than they do when attached to the main ice shelf. Greenland, a nation largely covered by ice, is also experiencing melting. Estimates as to how much ice will be lost vary, but the process is well under way.

Rising oceans will pose a threat to coastal cities and communities near the shore. However, cities and communities can adapt to rising waters. For instance, the cities of New Orleans and Amsterdam are already below sea level. They use a series of dikes, canals, levees, and

# Climate Change in the Developing World

The air in Shanghai, China, is heavily polluted. Sometimes the air quality is so bad that people are advised to stay indoors.

In the new millennium, emerging nations such as China and India have risen as impressive world powers with thriving economies. As a developing nation with an enormous manufacturing industry, China has in the past prioritized economic expansion over protecting the environment, though its policies have been changing in recent years. China is the globe's largest consumer of coal and the top producer of carbon dioxide emissions from fossil fuels and industry.

India, another developing nation that consumes a great deal of coal, also poses a threat to Earth's climate. Currently, India is the second most populous nation in the world, and its population is estimated to overtake China's in the coming decades. While India produces just 7 percent of all global carbon emissions, it is still the fourth-largest producer in the world.

drainage systems to control the water. In the case of Hurricane Katrina in 2005, the nation witnessed the dire consequences of such defenses failing in New Orleans. If global sea levels rise the way they are projected to, cities such as New York may eventually be below sea level, too. Just as Amsterdam and New Orleans have managed to survive (sometimes just barely) while being surrounded by potentially flooding waters, so, too, will many other cities be affected by rising oceans.

We know that the oceans are becoming acidic, but we don't yet know the extent to which this will affect marine life. While very acidic oceans would be fatal to many ocean species, the oceans are acidifying very gradually. Since this process is the result of the oceans absorbing atmospheric carbon, a reduction in the amount of carbon we put into the air might be able to slow, stop, or even reverse the trend. Some species may even have time to adapt to higher levels of acidification.

# REGIONAL IMPACTS

Climate change will have different effects on different regions of the world. In the United States, coastal communities will have to contend with flooding, which may result in serious losses and displacements. Higher temperatures and heat waves will particularly affect cities, which are already several degrees warmer on average than suburban or rural areas. This will be true for all of North America.

In South America, the impact of climate change on the Amazon rain forest and other tropical areas could be significant. The rain forest is a vital component of the carbon cycle. The lush vegetation, home to millions of animal and plant species, also absorbs a great deal of atmospheric carbon each and every day. Many of the animals living in the rain forest are sensitive to environmental changes, and there is a strong possibility that many could become extinct in the coming decades. The area faces serious problems with deforestation as a result of human expansion. If drought were to cause the Amazon rain forest to die off, it could release into the atmosphere the ninety billion tons of carbon it currently stores.

In Africa, water stress will be far more pronounced. Changing weather could make things difficult for nonirrigated agriculture, which is agriculture that relies on direct rainfall rather than pumped-in water supplies from aquifers or reservoirs. Small or failed harvests would place enormous stress on food supplies. Increased land aridity (dryness) might also negatively impact agriculture and food production.

Much of Asia will be heavily impacted by climate change, especially when it comes to drinking water. The IPCC estimates that fresh water will become increasingly scarce by 2050. Asia's large population— approximately four billion people—means that water stress will have a serious impact on the continent. Flooding and the spread of disease, especially water-borne disease, will also pose a threat to Asia's population.

Australia, New Zealand, and the Pacific Islands will almost certainly experience wildlife extinction, especially among offshore coral reefs. Droughts and increased aridity could impact agriculture and lead to an increase in forest fires. Some offshore islands in the Pacific Ocean could have their landmasses reduced by the rising sea level, or could even disappear completely.

# ADAPTING TO A CHANGING CLIMATE

It is believed that one of the reasons that heat waves caused so many deaths in Europe in 2003 is that many Europeans weren't used to such high temperatures and, therefore, weren't knowledgeable about ways to cope. With the proper preparations, far fewer people would succumb to the heat. As climate change continues, we will have to find ways to adapt to our new world.

According to the IPCC, we can help offset the effects of climate change in a variety of ways. For instance, water stress could be lessened by better management of our freshwater supplies (including lakes, rivers, and streams), wastewater reprocessing, and the use of desalinization technology to make saltwater drinkable. We can avoid aridity and desertification by planting more trees. More efficient farming techniques and crop irrigation can reduce food shortages. Public health initiatives can help avoid the spread of disease.

The threats to our environment and, in many places, people's basic way of life are real and pressing. There is little evidence that the survival of humanity as a whole is in immediate danger, but human-caused climate change will bring about considerable geographic, economic, and environmental changes if we don't work together to make some big changes.

# CHAPTER 4

# A GREENER FUTURE

Scientists, nations, and nongovernmental organizations around the world have been working together for decades to devise new solutions to the complicated problem of climate change. They have sought to achieve a delicate balance between environmental stewardship and human progress. Certainly, electricity, running water, and new modes of transportation—not to mention the countless other new technologies that seem to emerge on a daily basis—have improved the lives of billions of people. However, we can take these conveniences for granted and overuse precious resources. Encouraging more environmental awareness on every level of society has the potential to turn the tides of climate change—as does a combination of governmental regulation, international agreements and partnerships, and institutional support for greener technologies.

## SEEKING A GLOBAL SOLUTION

Realistically, any solution to climate change would have to be conducted on a global scale, with the full participation of all the world's nations and peoples. In 1997, the international community worked together to

Above: Environmental activists in Israel protest US president Donald Trump in 2017, shortly before he withdrew the United States from the Paris Agreement.

# Locally Sourced Foods

Foods that are grown and produced locally can be found at farmers' markets around the country.

Although many people may not think about it, the food that they buy in the grocery store is often no grown locally. We've become accustomed to getting any kind of food at any time of the year, whether it is in season or not. Demand for certain foods means that they are shipped in, often from very far away.

Transporting food long distances creates carbon emissions. You can avoid this by purchasing locally grown produce and other food products. Many communities have farmers' markets or farm stands where such products can be purchased. Buying locally sourced food not only benefits local farmers, it also helps you do your part to combat climate change by reducing greenhouse emissions create a piece of legislation that would coordinate countries worldwide in the fight against climate change. This legislation, known as the Kyoto Protocol, went into effect in 2005. While the United States did not sign the treaty, the majority of the world's countries did. Dozens of industrialized nations were required to cut greenhouse gas admissions, but developing countries, including India and China, were exempt.

In 2015, the so-called Paris Agreement replaced the Kyoto Protocol in many respects. Under this new pact, 196 countries committed to keep global warming from reaching 3.6°F (2°C) above preindustrial levels— and to limit it to 2.7°F (1.5°C) if possible. The Nature Conservancy called it "the first time ... that the world has agreed on a path forward." This time, China, which had been suffering severe air pollution problems, made a pledge to participate, and in November 2017, the *New York Times* reported that it was "well on track to meet the commitments it made under the Paris climate accord."

One big difference between the Paris Agreement and previous efforts was that nations didn't have to decide on a one-size-fits-all approach. Rather, each country can decide how to meet its commitment to lower greenhouse gas emissions, based on the unique challenges it faces. Many have declared the agreement a colossal step forward. However, even if the Paris Climate Agreement's goal of 3.6°F (2°C) is achieved, a study conducted and published in 2018 by the World Wildlife Fund found that ecologically diverse areas such as the Galapagos may still suffer a 25 percent loss in the species that live there.

In June 2017, the United States under the leadership of President Donald Trump chose to withdraw from the Paris Agreement, to which the Barack Obama administration had previously committed. Trump claimed that "the Paris deal hamstrings the United States while empowering some of the world's top polluting countries" and said he would aim to renegotiate it. However, a joint statement issued by Germany, France, and Italy indicated that it could not be renegotiated.

In response to the withdrawal, Obama, in a rare post-presidency statement, said that the United States had joined "a small handful of nations that reject the future." The Nature Conservancy called the decision "short-sighted," and more than twelve hundred governors, mayors, businesses, and universities around the United States reasserted their commitment to meet the standards of the agreement. Industry leaders, too, spoke out against the choice: "climate change is real," General Electric CEO Jeff Immelt said. According to nonprofit group Climate Interactive, without significant changes, the United States alone could warm the world by 0.5°F (0.3°C) by the year 2100.

## RENEWABLE ENERGY

More than 17 percent of electricity in the United States was already generated by renewable energy sources in 2017, according to the US Energy Information Administration. Hydropower led the way at 7.5 percent, followed by wind power at 6.3 percent, the burning of biomass (such as wood and solid waste) at 1.6 percent, and solar power at 1.3 percent. Some US states, including Washington, Oregon, and Hawaii, produce more than 95 percent of their power from renewable sources.

Solar power is among the most promising sources of green energy. It uses the sun's rays to generate electricity, making it a completely clean form of energy. Installing solar panels on the roof of a house can greatly reduce a homeowner's electric bill. Large solar collectors may someday power entire communities. This technology is still evolving, and the solar collectors of tomorrow could be much more efficient than the ones we have today.

Wind power is another source of clean energy. Although wind turbines can only function properly in parts of the country that enjoy steady and reliable winds, some states get up to 20 percent of their energy from wind power.

Hydroelectric power uses the power of rushing water to generate electricity. Like wind power, hydroelectric power on its own will probably never be a global solution to climate change. Not every waterway can be harnessed to generate hydropower, and not every region has access to ample, powerful, and moving water supplies. While hydroelectricity is a clean energy source, it can still cause ecological damage. Hydroelectric

Workers install a floating solar farm in Huainan, China, on a lake that was created when a coal mine collapsed and flooded.

dams, for example, can disturb the habitat of fish, bird, and animal species in the surrounding area. This is especially true in those areas that have been deprived of their usual water supplies following the dams' construction.

## NUCLEAR POWER

Often considered to be a dangerous source of energy, nuclear power is nevertheless put forth as a far cleaner, more abundant, and renewable source of energy than fossil fuels. About 20 percent of the United States' energy comes from nuclear power plants. France is perhaps the world's biggest user of nuclear power—it gets approximately 75 percent of its energy from nuclear power plants. However, in 2017, France's environment minister committed to closing as many as seventeen nuclear reactors by 2025, reducing the amount of energy sourced from nuclear to 50 percent. The goal was to comply with a renewable energy law in France.

While nuclear power doesn't generate greenhouse gases, it does create extraordinarily hazardous radioactive waste. Storing this waste can be a problem, as it poses a severe threat to anyone exposed to it, and it can leach into soil and groundwater. Nuclear power can also be very dangerous if something goes wrong at the power plant.

For instance, in 1986, the Chernobyl nuclear power plant in Ukraine experienced what is known as a nuclear meltdown. An error caused one of the reactors to explode, releasing radioactive material into the atmosphere. Much of it contaminated neighboring countries. To date, this has been the worst nuclear accident that the world has known. Fifty-six people died in the explosion itself, and as many as four thousand people may have eventually died of radiation sickness and radiation-related cancers. The area around the Chernobyl plant is still very radioactive.

With the proper oversight, nuclear power is considered to be perfectly safe. Unfortunately, there is no way to guarantee that nuclear power plants will not experience calamities on par with the Chernobyl disaster.

# WHAT YOU CAN DO

The clothes you wear, the hamburger you eat for dinner, and even the paper this book is printed on were created through processes that involved the production and emission of greenhouse gases. Nearly every single aspect of our way of life contributes to climate change. In short, every person on Earth contributes to the warming of the planet—and we can all join the effort to stop it.

Using public transportation or riding a bike to school and work can cut down on your carbon emissions. You can also purchase locally grown food or locally produced goods, such as clothing or other consumer items. Much of what we buy has traveled great distances to reach us, creating pollution in the process.

Many products that we buy every day are designed to be discarded. Newspapers, magazines, cardboard packaging, aluminum cans, and glass and plastic bottles are some things that can be easily recycled, rather than simply thrown away and dumped in a landfill. Recycling these products prevents waste, saves energy, and cuts down on the amount of greenhouse gas that would otherwise be used to manufacture new versions of these products from scratch.

By making the effort to conserve electricity at home, you can make a dent in your carbon emissions. The electricity that we use when turning

Every individual has a role to play in fighting pollution, reducing greenhouse gas emissions, and building a healthier planet.

on lights and appliances comes to us from power plants, which generate greenhouse gases. Remembering to turn off the lights when you leave a room and turn off and unplug electronic appliances when you go to sleep can dramatically reduce your carbon footprint.

If you want to take a more active role in preventing climate change, there's no reason not to start now. Plant a garden, convince your parents to buy highly efficient compact fluorescent light bulbs, recycle regularly, and learn how to effectively winterize your home to save energy. You can also see what kinds of organizations or clubs your school or community has that are devoted to environmental causes. If there isn't one, start one!

If you're interested in learning more, take an environmental science course. Opportunities for careers related to energy, especially the next wave of renewable energy technology, are growing. Between 2015 and 2016, renewable energy employment in the United States grew almost 18 percent—much faster than average job growth. Anything you can do to secure the future of the planet will assure your own future health and well-being, and that of every generation that comes after you.

# GLOSSARY

**acidification**  The process by which something becomes more acidic. In the case of Earth's oceans, an intake of carbon dioxide causes the water to become more acidic.

**aridity**  A lack of moisture.

**atmosphere**  The layers of gases surrounding Earth.

**carbon dioxide**  A greenhouse gas.

**climate change**  A shift in climate patterns, either globally or regionally; can be caused by natural or human factors.

**drought**  A prolonged shortage of water.

**emission**  Something released as a result of certain processes. For instance, cars emit carbon dioxide as exhaust, and the uranium used in nuclear power plants emits radiation as it decays.

**endemic**  Native only to one particular area of the world.

**extinction**  The death of every single organism of a certain species of plant or animal.

**famine**  A mass food shortage resulting in widespread hunger.

**fluctuations**  Variations in something that can be measured, such as temperature.

**fossil fuels**  Nonrenewable energy sources (including coal, methane, and petroleum) that contain a high percentage of carbon or hydrocarbon and are formed by the decomposition of buried dead organisms over hundreds of millions of years. When burned to generate energy, they emit carbon dioxide into the atmosphere.

**global warming**  A gradual increase in the temperature of the Earth's overall atmosphere, often attributed to the greenhouse effect.

**greenhouse effect**  A process by which heat from the sun is trapped inside of the Earth's atmosphere; amplified by the emission of such greenhouse gases as carbon dioxide and methane.

**levee**  A dam used to keep an area from flooding.

**livestock**  Cattle, pigs, sheep, and other domestic farm animals that are raised to be consumed as food or sold for profit.

**marine**  Having to do with the sea. Marine animals are those that spend their lives in oceans, lakes, or rivers.

**methane**  A greenhouse gas.

**migration**  The mass movement of groups of people or animals from one location to another.

**renewable energy**  Energy produced by a source that, when used, is not irrevocably depleted.

# FURTHER INFORMATION

## BOOKS

Kolbert, Elizabeth. *The Sixth Extinction: An Unnatural History*. New York: Henry Holt and Company, 2014.

Thiele, Leslie Paul. *Sustainability (Key Concepts)*. Malden, MA: Polity Press, 2016.

Wilson, Edward O. *Half-Earth: Our Planet's Fight for Life*. New York: Liveright Publishing Corporation, 2016.

Withgott, Jay H., and Matthew Laposata. *Essential Environment: The Science Behind the Stories*. New York: Pearson, 2014.

## WEBSITES

### Center for Climate and Energy Solutions

https://www.c2es.org

This nonprofit, nonpartisan organization offers useful information on the basics of climate science and policy, as well as up-to-date reports on environmental topics from around the world.

### Climate Change: US Global Change Research Program

https://www.globalchange.gov/climate-change

This website, operated by a US governmental organization, offers a complete explanation of climate change along with data, resources, and multimedia on the topic.

### Global Climate Change: Vital Signs of the Planet

https://climate.nasa.gov

This useful resource, operated by the National Aeronautics and Space Administration (NASA), offers the latest information on carbon dioxide concentration in the atmosphere, the status of arctic ice, and global initiatives for environmental protection.

# VIDEOS

## A Way Forward: Facing Climate Change

https://video.nationalgeographic.com/video/way-forward-climate
This *National Geographic* video shows footage from around
the world as it explains the effects of climate change and what
scientists recommend doing next.

## Climate Change with Bill Nye

https://video.nationalgeographic.com/video/news/101-
videos/151201-climate-change-bill-nye-news
Bill Nye, the Science Guy, explains how each of us can do our part
to mitigate climate change.

## Plastics 101

https://video.nationalgeographic.com/ib.adnxs.com/
seg?add=1&redir=https%3A%2F%2Fvideo.nationalgeographic.
com%2Fvideo%2F101-videos%2Fplastics-101
This *National Geographic* video explains the devastating impacts
that plastics are having on the planet.

# ORGANIZATIONS

## Environment and Climate Change Canada

12th floor, Fontaine Building
200 Sacré-Coeur Boulevard
Gatineau, QC K1A 0H3
(819) 938-3860
https://www.canada.ca/en/environment-climate-change.html
ECCC is committed to disseminating important information about
the conservation of Canada's natural environment and sustainable
practices for doing so.

## Environmental Defence

116 Spadina Ave., Suite 300
Toronto, ON M5V 2K6
(416) 323-9521
http://www.environmentaldefence.ca
This Canadian organization promotes environmental protection
and green initiatives on both the individual and institutional levels.

## Intergovernmental Panel on Climate Change

c/o World Meteorological Organization
7bis Avenue de la Paix
C. P. 2300
CH- 1211 Geneva 2, Switzerland
+41-22-730-8208
http://www.ipcc.ch
The IPCC is comprised of a comprehensive group of climate change experts. The IPCC offers scientific data and reports along with key information on international efforts to battle climate change.

### Nature Conservancy

4245 North Fairfax Drive, Suite 100
Arlington, VA 22203-1606
(703) 841-5300
http://www.nature.org
his conservation organization identifies principal threats to marine life, freshwater ecosystems, forests, and protected areas, and then uses a scientific approach to save them.

## Sierra Club

2101 Webster St., Suite 1300
Oakland, CA 94612
(415) 977-5500
http://www.sierraclub.org
Founded in 1892 by conservationist John Muir, the Serra Club is the United States' oldest environmental organization.

### United States Environmental Protection Agency

1200 Pennsylvania Avenue NW
Washington, DC 20460
(800) 438-2474
http://www.epa.gov
Founded in 1970, the EPA works to shape US environmental policy.

# BIBLIOGRAPHY

"Agriculture: Climate." United States Environmental Protection Agency. Accessed May 14, 2018. https://www.epa.gov/agriculture/agriculture-climate.

American Geophysical Union. "Global Warming Could Release Trillions of Pounds of Carbon Annually from East Siberia's Vast Frozen Soils." *ScienceDaily*, June 12, 2008. http://www.sciencedaily.com/releases/2008/06/080611154839.htm.

American Institute of Biological Sciences. "Thawing Permafrost Likely to Boost Global Warming, New Assessment Concludes." *ScienceDaily*, September 2, 2008. http://www.sciencedaily.com/releases/2008/09/080901084854.htm.

Associated Press. "Scientists Warn of Water Shortages and Disease Linked to Global Warming." *New York Times*, March 12, 2007. http://www.nytimes.com/2007/03/12/science/earth/12climate.html.

Barkham, Patrick. "The 10 Species Most at Risk from Climate Change." *Guardian* (UK), January 19, 2017. https://www.theguardian.com/environment/2017/jan/19/critical-10-species-at-risk-climate-change-endangered-world.

Bernstein, Lenny, et al. "Climate Change 2007: Synthesis Report — Summary for Policymakers." Intergovernmental Panel on Climate Change, November 17, 2007. http://www.ipcc.ch/pdf/assessment-report/ar4/syr/ar4_syr_spm.pdf.

"Birds." International Union for Conservation of Nature. Accessed May 14, 2018. https://www.iucn.org/theme/species/our-work/birds.

Bradsher, Keith. "China to Pass U.S. in 2009 in Emissions." *New York Times*, November 7, 2006. http://www.nytimes.com/2006/11/07/business/worldbusiness/07pollute.html.

Bradsher, Keith, and David Barboza. "Pollution from Chinese Coal Casts a Global Shadow." *New York Times*, June 11, 2006. http://www.nytimes.com/2006/06/11/business/worldbusiness/11chinacoal.html.

Brown, Paul. "Global Warming Is Killing Us, Too, Say Inuit." *Guardian* (UK), December 11, 2003. http://www.guardian.co.uk/environment/2003/dec/11/weather.climatechange.

"Certainty vs. Uncertainty: Understanding Scientific Terms About Climate Change." Union of Concerned Scientists. Accessed May 14, 2018. https://www.ucsusa.org/global-warming/science-and-impacts/science/certainty-vs-uncertainty.html#.WvnHBS_MyL4.

"Climate Action." World Food Programme. Accessed May 14, 2018. http://www1.wfp.org/climate-action.

Clover, Charles. "IPCC: Lawson Wrong About Climate Change." *Telegraph* (UK), November 10, 2008. http://www.telegraph.co.uk/earth/earthcomment/charlesclover/3339514/IPCC-Lawson-wrong-about-climate-change.html.

CNN Library. "Kyoto Protocol Fast Facts." CNN, March 21, 2018. https://www.cnn.com/2013/07/26/world/kyoto-protocol-fast-facts/index.html.

Core Writing Team, Rajendra K. Pachauri, and Leo Meyer. *Climate Change 2014: Synthesis Report.* Intergovernmental Panel on Climate Change, 2014. http://www.ipcc.ch/pdf/assessment-report/ar5/syr/AR5_SYR_FINAL_Front_matters.pdf.

Davey, Melissa. "Humans Causing Climate to Change 170 Times Faster Than Natural Forces." *Guardian* (UK), February 12, 2017. https://www.theguardian.com/environment/2017/feb/12/humans-causing-climate-to-change-170-times-faster-than-natural-forces.

Del Bello, Lou. "Globalisation and Global Warming Threaten Inuit Food Security." *Rethink*, October 12, 2017. https://rethink.earth/globalisation-and-global-warming-threaten-inuit-food-security.

Dessler, Andrew E., and Edward A. Parson. *The Science and Politics of Global Climate Change: A Guide to the Debate.* New York: Cambridge University Press, 2006.

Dow, Kristin, and Thomas Downing. *The Atlas of Climate Change: Mapping the World's Greatest Challenge*. Berkeley, CA: University of California Press, 2007.

Eilperin, Juliet. "Growing Acidity of Oceans May Kill Corals." *Washington Post*, July 5, 2006. http://www.washingtonpost.com/ wp-dyn/content/article/2006/07/04/AR2006070400772.html.

Emanuel, Kerry. *What We Know About Climate Change*. Cambridge, MA: MIT Press, 2007.

"Extinction Crisis Continues Apace." International Union for Conservation of Nature, November 3, 2009. https://www.iucn. org/content/extinction-crisis-continues-apace.

"Global Greenhouse Gas Emissions Data." United States Environmental Protection Agency. Accessed May 14, 2018. https:// www.epa.gov/ghgemissions/global-greenhouse-gas-emissions-data.

"Global Warming and Hurricanes." Geophysical Fluid Dynamics Laboratory, April 25, 2018. https://www.gfdl.noaa.gov/global-warming-and-hurricanes.

"Half of Plant and Animal Species at Risk from Climate Change in World's Most Important Natural Places." World Wildlife Fund, March 14, 2018. https://www.worldwildlife.org/ press-releases/half-of-plant-and-animal-species-at-risk-from-climate-change-in-world-s-most-important-natural-places.

Holder, Josh, Niko Kommenda, and Jonathan Watts. "The Three-Degree World: The Cities That Will Be Drowned by Global Warming." *Guardian* (UK), November 3, 2017. https://www.theguardian.com/cities/ng-interactive/2017/ nov/03/three-degree-world-cities-drowned-global-warming.

Houghton, John. *Global Warming: The Complete Briefing*. New York: Cambridge University Press, 2004.

Hurst, Alexander. "France Could Close 'Up to 17' Nuclear Reactors by 2025." France 24, July 12, 2017. http://www.france24. com/en/20170710-france-hulot-could-close-nuclear-plants.

"The IUCN Red List of Threatened Species." International Union for Conservation of Nature, 2015. https://cmsdocs. s3.amazonaws.com/keydocuments/IUCN_Red_List_Bro-chure_2015_LOW.pdf.

Joyce, Christopher. "Massive Government Report Says Climate Is Warming and Humans Are the Cause." *NPR*, November 2, 2017. https://www.npr.org/sections/thet-wo-way/2017/11/02/561608576/massive-government-report-says-climate-is-warming-and-humans-are-the-cause.

Kasnoff, Craig. "Endangered Earth: Promoting the Plight of Endangered Species and the Efforts to Save Them." *Endangered Earth*. Accessed May 14, 2018. http://www.endangered-earth.com

Lean, Geoffrey, and Fred Pearce. "Amazon Rainforest 'Could Become a Desert.'" *Independent* (UK), July 23, 2006. http://www.independent.co.uk/environment/amazon-rainfor-est-could-become-a-desert-408977.html.

Lopez, Daniel. "Fact Sheet: Jobs in Renewable Energy and Energy Efficiency (2017)." Environmental and Energy Study Institute, February 15, 2017. http://www.eesi.org/papers/view/fact-sheet-jobs-in-renewable-energy-and-energy-efficiency-2017.

Maasch, Kirk A. "Cracking the Big Chill." Nova Online. Retrieved April 2009. http://www.pbs.org/wgbh/nova/ice/chill.html.

"Mammals on the IUCN Red List." International Union for Conservation of Nature, IUCN Ted List of Threatened Species. Accessed May 14, 2018. http://www.iucnredlist.org/initiatives/mammals/analysis/red-list-status.

McKie, Robin. "Scientists to Issue Stark Warning over Dramatic New Sea Level Figures." *Guardian* (UK), March 8, 2009. http://www.guardian.co.uk/science/2009/mar/08/cli-mate-change-flooding.

Milman, Oliver, David Smith, and Damian Carrington. "Donald Trump Confirms US Will Quit Paris Climate Agreement." *Guardian* (UK), June 1, 2017. https://www.theguardian.com/environment/2017/jun/01/donald-trump-confirms-us-will-quit-paris-climate-deal.

Mooney, Chris. "Is Climate Change Causing an Upsurge in U.S. Tornadoes?" *New Scientist*, July 30, 2008. http://www.newscientist.com/article/mg19926671.800-is-climate-change-causing-an-upsurge-in-us-tornadoes.html.

Parker, Laura. "Sea Level Rise Will Flood Hundreds of Cities in the Near Future." *National Geographic*, July 12, 2017. https://news.nationalgeographic.com/2017/07/sea-level-rise-flood-global-warming-science/#close.

Quinn, Ben. "China's Carbon Dioxide Production Soars." *Telegraph* (UK), June 20, 2007. http://www.telegraph.co.uk/earth/earthnews/3298031/Chinas-carbon-dioxide-production-soars.html.

"Renewable Energy Production by State." US Department of Energy. Accessed May 16, 2018. https://www.energy.gov/maps/renewable-energy-production-state.

Resnick, Brian. "An Iceberg the Size of Delaware Has Broken off from Antarctica." *Vox*, July 12, 2017. https://www.vox.com/science-and-health/2017/7/12/15947448/antarctica-ice-berg-larsen-c-how-big.

"Scientific Consensus: Earth's Climate Is Warming." NASA, Global Climate Change, Vital Signs of the Planet. Accessed May 14, 2018. https://climate.nasa.gov/scientific-consensus.

Sengupta, Somini. "Why China Wants to Lead on Climate, but Clings to Coal (for Now)." *New York Times*, November 14, 2017. https://www.nytimes.com/2017/11/14/climate/china-coal.html.

Sharp, Tim. "What Is Earth's Average Temperature?" Space.com, April 23, 2018. https://www.space.com/17816-earth-temperature.html.

"Sources of Greenhouse Gas Emissions." United States Environmental Protection Agency. Accessed May 16, 2018. https://www.epa.gov/ghgemissions/sources-greenhouse-gas-emissions.

"Study: Climate Change Soon to Be Main Cause of Heat Waves in West, Great Lakes." National Oceanic and Atmospheric Administration, March 19, 2018. http://www.noaa.gov/news/study-climate-change-soon-to-be-main-cause-of-heat-waves-in-west-great-lakes.

"The 10 Hottest Global Years on Record." Climate Central, January 18, 2018. http://www.climatecentral.org/gallery/graphics/the-10-hottest-global-years-on-record.

"10 Things You Should Know about the Paris Agreement, and What They Mean for You." Nature Conservancy. Accessed May 16, 2018. https://www.nature.org/ourinitiatives/urgentissues/global-warming-climate-change/the-paris-agreement-what-does-it-mean.xml.

"U.S. Tornado Climatology." National Centers for Environmental Information, National Oceanic and Atmospheric Administration. Accessed May 14, 2018. https://www.ncdc.noaa.gov/climate-information/extreme-events/us-tornado-climatology.

"The Water Crisis." Water.org. Accessed May 14, 2018. https://water.org/our-impact/water-crisis.

"What Is U.S. Electricity Generation by Energy Source?" US Energy Information Administration, March 7, 2018. https://www.eia.gov/tools/faqs/faq.php?id=427&t=3.

# INDEX

# ABOUT THE AUTHOR

**Erin L. McCoy** is a literature, language, and cultural studies educator and poet. She has won several awards for her investigative reporting on fossil fuels, climate change, and alternative energy. She holds a master of arts degree in Hispanic studies and a master of fine arts in creative writing from the University of Washington. She has edited nearly twenty nonfiction books for young adults, including *The Mexican-American War* and *The Israel-Palestine Border Conflict* from the Redrawing the Map series with Cavendish Square Publishing. She grew up learning about climate change from her father, Doug McCoy, who is an environmental science educator. She is from Louisville, Kentucky.